Autor und Illustrationen: Michael Junga
Druck und Verarbeitung: westermann druck GmbH, Braunschweig
ISBN 3-89414-607-9

It's easy to play with bambinoLÜK:

Open the bambinoLÜK control unit und place it on the open bambino LÜK workbook. Put the six tiles symbol side up on the exercises with the same symbol, for example the tile with the red symbol 'house' on the exercise with the red symbol 'house' on the upper left hand corner.
When you have placed all the tiles on the exercises, take up the tile with the symbol 'house' and look at the exercise on which it was placed. Which picture underneath matches it? Put the tile on the matching picture. Repeat for the other five tiles and exercises. Close the bambinoLÜK control unit and turn it over. Now you can see the pattern made by the six tiles.

Everything OK?
And now have fun !

Jouer avec ba
tout simple:

Ouvre l'unité d
LÜK et place-la
LÜK ouvert. Pla
boles découver
avec les symbo
donc la carte s
son» sur l'exer
rouge «maison
Quand tu as pl
prends la carte
tu examines l'e
Quelle image s
respond à cet e
sur l'image cor
de la même faç
tes et exercices
l'unité de contr
tourne-la vers l
peux comparer
tion avec celui

Tout est exact
avec bambino LÜK !

1

2

4

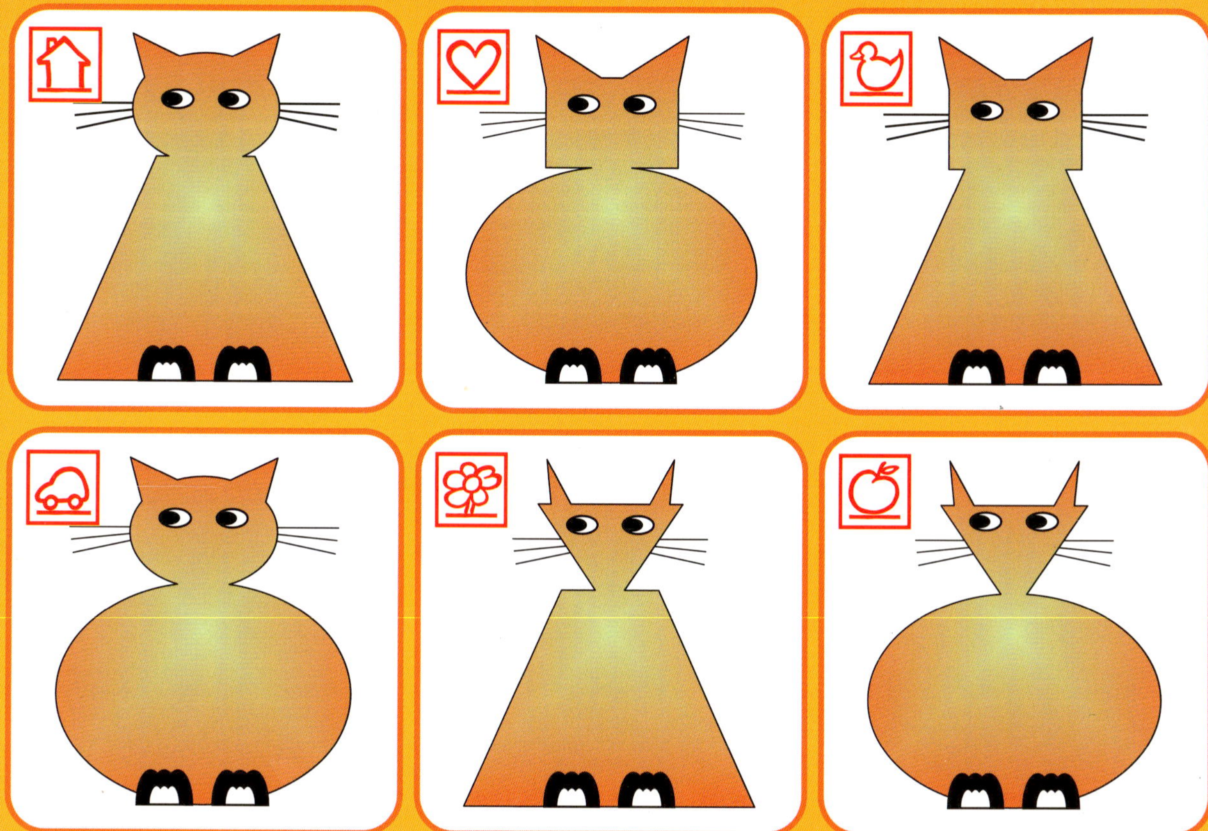

5

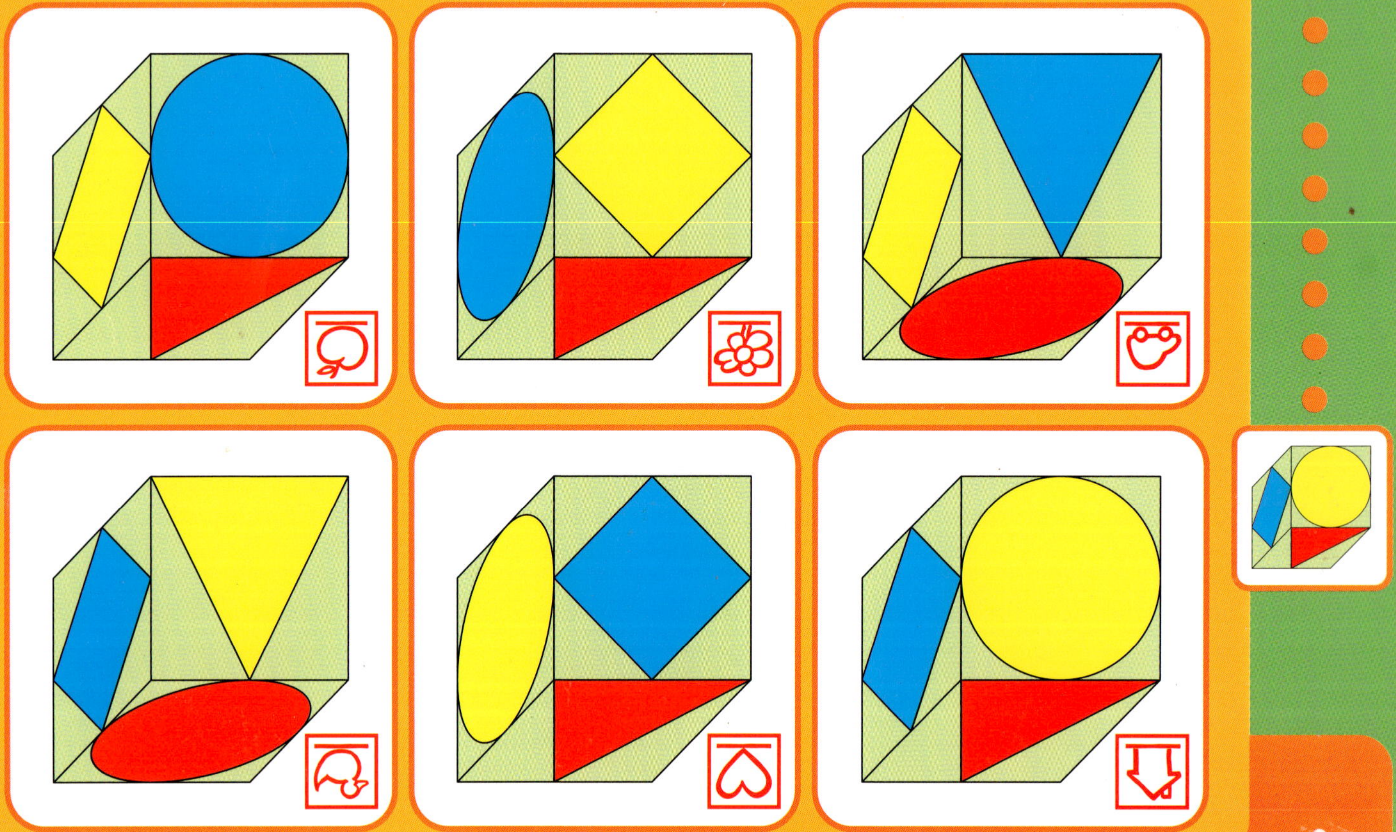

8

11

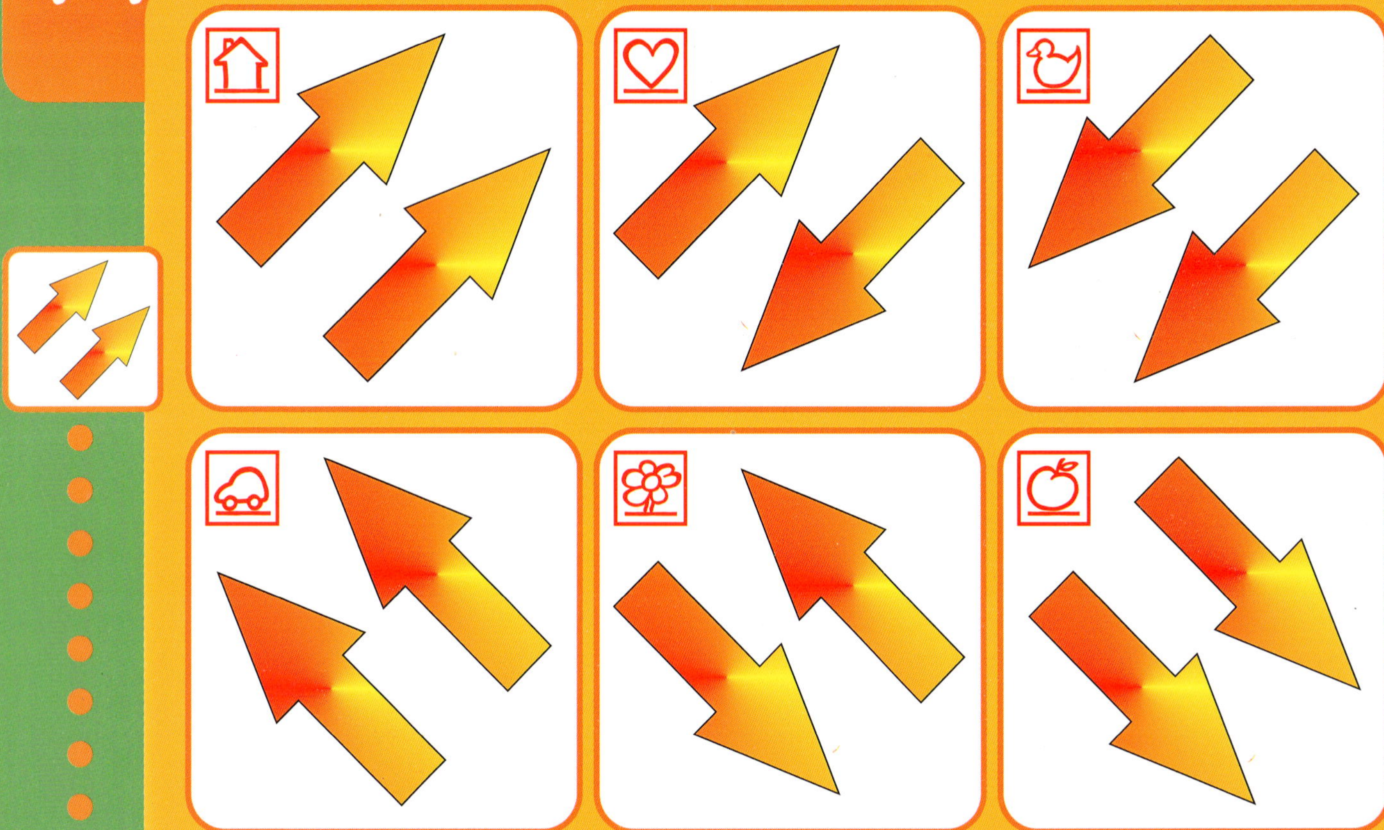

Inhalt Content Table des matières Índice

Alle Übungen haben klare Farben, eindeutige Formen und kindgemäße Bilder. Sie trainieren die Wahrnehmungsfähigkeit der Kinder und helfen ihnen, Gleiches zuzuordnen und Ähnliches voneinander zu unterscheiden.

All the exercises are illustrated in clear colours and plain shapes. They are designed to train the faculty of perception in children and help them to differentiate between identical and similar objects.